The Busy Entrepreneur Series: Organization

This calendar was created for Scrubbs Quality Cleaning, Inc. in Brevard County Florida. The owner is an incredible entrepreneur who got left out of the techy world and was struggling with finding a calendar that had enough space and enough area to write, and make notes.

Many Busy Entrepreneurs struggle with finding the "right" organization system. As long as you have an organizational system, it is the right one. Sure, you can always work on efficiency; however, you want to make sure you have something that works, that you can improve on.

Start with this paper system. If you would like a tutorial on how to use this for your business more effectively contact Business Resolutions at Ellen@BusinessResolutions.org or simply call 321-243-7543 and leave a message.

I wish Prosperity to all you are involved with. I wish you a successful career as an entrepreneur. More importantly, please ask for help when you need it. – We all need it!

Ellen Onieal Little

Weekly Planner

Week Beginning: [　　　]

Month:

Important

Notes

☑	ABC	Prioritized Task List

Date	People to Call

Monday
1
2
3
4
5
6
7
8
9
10
11

Wednesday

1
2
3
4
5
6
7
8
9
10
11

Friday
1
2
3
4
5
6
7
8
9
10
11

Tuesday
1
2
3
4
5
6
7
8
9
10
11

Thursday

1
2
3
4
5
6
7
8
9
10
11

Saturday

1
2
3
4
5
6

Sunday

1
2
3
4
5
6

Date: [   ]   Start Day: [   ]

Day:

_____

	Reminders
-	
-	
-	
-	
-	
-	
-	
-	
-	
-	

☑	ABC	Prioritized Task List

Time	People to Call

$Amt	Expenses

Appointments

Time	
7 :00	
:30	
8 :00	
:15	
:30	
:45	
9 :00	
:15	
:30	
:45	
10 :00	
:15	
:30	
:45	
11 :00	
:15	
:30	
:45	
12 :00	
:15	
:30	
:45	
1 :00	
:15	
:30	
:45	
2 :00	
:15	
:30	
:45	
3 :00	
:15	
:30	
:45	
4 :00	
:15	
:30	
:45	
5 :00	
:30	
6 :00	
:30	
7 :00	
:30	
8 :00	
:30	
9 :00	
:30	

Date: [   ]   Start Day: [   ]

Day:

_____

Reminders
-
-
-
-
-
-
-
-
-
-

☑	ABC	Prioritized Task List

Time	People to Call

$Amt	Expenses

Appointments

7	:00
	:30
8	:00
	:15
	:30
	:45
9	:00
	:15
	:30
	:45
10	:00
	:15
	:30
	:45
11	:00
	:15
	:30
	:45
12	:00
	:15
	:30
	:45
1	:00
	:15
	:30
	:45
2	:00
	:15
	:30
	:45
3	:00
	:15
	:30
	:45
4	:00
	:15
	:30
	:45
5	:00
	:30
6	:00
	:30
7	:00
	:30
8	:00
	:30
9	:00
	:30

Date: [   ]   Start Day: [   ]

Day:

_____

Reminders
-
-
-
-
-
-
-
-
-
-

☑	ABC	Prioritized Task List

Time	People to Call

$Amt	Expenses

Appointments

7 :00	
:30	
8 :00	
:15	
:30	
:45	
9 :00	
:15	
:30	
:45	
10 :00	
:15	
:30	
:45	
11 :00	
:15	
:30	
:45	
12 :00	
:15	
:30	
:45	
1 :00	
:15	
:30	
:45	
2 :00	
:15	
:30	
:45	
3 :00	
:15	
:30	
:45	
4 :00	
:15	
:30	
:45	
5 :00	
:30	
6 :00	
:30	
7 :00	
:30	
8 :00	
:30	
9 :00	
:30	

Date: [ ]   Start Day: [ ]

Day:

_____

Reminders
- _____
- _____
- _____
- _____
- _____
- _____
- _____
- _____
- _____
- _____

☑	ABC	Prioritized Task List

Time	People to Call

$Amt	Expenses

Appointments

7 :00	
:30	
8 :00	
:15	
:30	
:45	
9 :00	
:15	
:30	
:45	
10 :00	
:15	
:30	
:45	
11 :00	
:15	
:30	
:45	
12 :00	
:15	
:30	
:45	
1 :00	
:15	
:30	
:45	
2 :00	
:15	
:30	
:45	
3 :00	
:15	
:30	
:45	
4 :00	
:15	
:30	
:45	
5 :00	
:30	
6 :00	
:30	
7 :00	
:30	
8 :00	
:30	
9 :00	
:30	

Date: [ ]   Start Day: [ ]

Day:

Reminders
-
-
-
-
-
-
-
-
-
-

☑	ABC	Prioritized Task List

Time	People to Call

$Amt	Expenses

Appointments	
7	:00
	:30
8	:00
	:15
	:30
	:45
9	:00
	:15
	:30
	:45
10	:00
	:15
	:30
	:45
11	:00
	:15
	:30
	:45
12	:00
	:15
	:30
	:45
1	:00
	:15
	:30
	:45
2	:00
	:15
	:30
	:45
3	:00
	:15
	:30
	:45
4	:00
	:15
	:30
	:45
5	:00
	:30
6	:00
	:30
7	:00
	:30
8	:00
	:30
9	:00
	:30

Date: [   ]   Start Day: [   ]

Day:

Reminders		Appointments

Reminders

- _____
- _____
- _____
- _____
- _____
- _____
- _____
- _____
- _____
- _____

☑	ABC	**Prioritized Task List**

Time	**People to Call**

$Amt	**Expenses**

Appointments

7	:00	
	:30	
8	:00	
	:15	
	:30	
	:45	
9	:00	
	:15	
	:30	
	:45	
10	:00	
	:15	
	:30	
	:45	
11	:00	
	:15	
	:30	
	:45	
12	:00	
	:15	
	:30	
	:45	
1	:00	
	:15	
	:30	
	:45	
2	:00	
	:15	
	:30	
	:45	
3	:00	
	:15	
	:30	
	:45	
4	:00	
	:15	
	:30	
	:45	
5	:00	
	:30	
6	:00	
	:30	
7	:00	
	:30	
8	:00	
	:30	
9	:00	
	:30	

Date: [   ]   Start Day: [   ]

Day:

Reminders		Appointments

Reminders

- _____
- _____
- _____
- _____
- _____
- _____
- _____
- _____
- _____
- _____

☑	ABC	**Prioritized Task List**

Time	**People to Call**

$Amt	**Expenses**

Appointments

7 :00	
:30	
8 :00	
:15	
:30	
:45	
9 :00	
:15	
:30	
:45	
10 :00	
:15	
:30	
:45	
11 :00	
:15	
:30	
:45	
12 :00	
:15	
:30	
:45	
1 :00	
:15	
:30	
:45	
2 :00	
:15	
:30	
:45	
3 :00	
:15	
:30	
:45	
4 :00	
:15	
:30	
:45	
5 :00	
:30	
6 :00	
:30	
7 :00	
:30	
8 :00	
:30	
9 :00	
:30	

Week Beginning: [ ]

Month:

Important

Notes

☑	ABC	Prioritized Task List

Date	People to Call

Monday
1
2
3
4
5
6
7
8
9
10
11

Wednesday

1
2
3
4
5
6
7
8
9
10
11

Friday
1
2
3
4
5
6
7
8
9
10
11

Tuesday
1
2
3
4
5
6
7
8
9
10
11

Thursday

1
2
3
4
5
6
7
8
9
10
11

Saturday

1
2
3
4
5
6

Sunday

1
2
3
4
5
6

Date: [   ]   Start Day: [   ]

Day:

_____

Reminders
-
-
-
-
-
-
-
-
-
-

☑	ABC	Prioritized Task List

Time	People to Call

$Amt	Expenses

Appointments

7	:00
	:30
8	:00
	:15
	:30
	:45
9	:00
	:15
	:30
	:45
10	:00
	:15
	:30
	:45
11	:00
	:15
	:30
	:45
12	:00
	:15
	:30
	:45
1	:00
	:15
	:30
	:45
2	:00
	:15
	:30
	:45
3	:00
	:15
	:30
	:45
4	:00
	:15
	:30
	:45
5	:00
	:30
6	:00
	:30
7	:00
	:30
8	:00
	:30
9	:00
	:30

Date: [   ]   Start Day: [   ]

Day:

_____

Reminders
-
-
-
-
-
-
-
-
-
-

☑	ABC	Prioritized Task List

Time	People to Call

$Amt	Expenses

Appointments	
7 :00	
:30	
8 :00	
:15	
:30	
:45	
9 :00	
:15	
:30	
:45	
10 :00	
:15	
:30	
:45	
11 :00	
:15	
:30	
:45	
12 :00	
:15	
:30	
:45	
1 :00	
:15	
:30	
:45	
2 :00	
:15	
:30	
:45	
3 :00	
:15	
:30	
:45	
4 :00	
:15	
:30	
:45	
5 :00	
:30	
6 :00	
:30	
7 :00	
:30	
8 :00	
:30	
9 :00	
:30	

Date: ☐   Start Day: ☐

Day:

Reminders		Appointments
-	7 :00	
-	:30	
-	8 :00	
-	:15	
-	:30	
-	:45	
-	9 :00	
-	:15	
-	:30	
-	:45	

☑	ABC	Prioritized Task List

Time	People to Call

$Amt	Expenses

Appointments (continued):

10 :00	
:15	
:30	
:45	
11 :00	
:15	
:30	
:45	
12 :00	
:15	
:30	
:45	
1 :00	
:15	
:30	
:45	
2 :00	
:15	
:30	
:45	
3 :00	
:15	
:30	
:45	
4 :00	
:15	
:30	
:45	
5 :00	
:30	
6 :00	
:30	
7 :00	
:30	
8 :00	
:30	
9 :00	
:30	

Date: [   ]   Start Day: [   ]

Day:

_____

	Reminders
-	_____
-	_____
-	_____
-	_____
-	_____
-	_____
-	_____
-	_____
-	_____
-	_____

☑	ABC	Prioritized Task List

Time	People to Call

$Amt	Expenses

Appointments

Time	
7 :00	
:30	
8 :00	
:15	
:30	
:45	
9 :00	
:15	
:30	
:45	
10 :00	
:15	
:30	
:45	
11 :00	
:15	
:30	
:45	
12 :00	
:15	
:30	
:45	
1 :00	
:15	
:30	
:45	
2 :00	
:15	
:30	
:45	
3 :00	
:15	
:30	
:45	
4 :00	
:15	
:30	
:45	
5 :00	
:30	
6 :00	
:30	
7 :00	
:30	
8 :00	
:30	
9 :00	
:30	

Date: [ ]   Start Day: [ ]

Day:

	Reminders	

Reminders
-
-
-
-
-
-
-
-
-
-

☑	ABC	Prioritized Task List

Time	People to Call

$Amt	Expenses

Appointments

7	:00	
	:30	
8	:00	
	:15	
	:30	
	:45	
9	:00	
	:15	
	:30	
	:45	
10	:00	
	:15	
	:30	
	:45	
11	:00	
	:15	
	:30	
	:45	
12	:00	
	:15	
	:30	
	:45	
1	:00	
	:15	
	:30	
	:45	
2	:00	
	:15	
	:30	
	:45	
3	:00	
	:15	
	:30	
	:45	
4	:00	
	:15	
	:30	
	:45	
5	:00	
	:30	
6	:00	
	:30	
7	:00	
	:30	
8	:00	
	:30	
9	:00	
	:30	

Date: [   ]   Start Day: [   ]

Day:

_____

Reminders		**Appointments**	

Reminders
- _____
- _____
- _____
- _____
- _____
- _____
- _____
- _____
- _____
- _____

☑	ABC	**Prioritized Task List**

Time	**People to Call**

$Amt	**Expenses**

Appointments

7	:00	
	:30	
8	:00	
	:15	
	:30	
	:45	
9	:00	
	:15	
	:30	
	:45	
10	:00	
	:15	
	:30	
	:45	
11	:00	
	:15	
	:30	
	:45	
12	:00	
	:15	
	:30	
	:45	
1	:00	
	:15	
	:30	
	:45	
2	:00	
	:15	
	:30	
	:45	
3	:00	
	:15	
	:30	
	:45	
4	:00	
	:15	
	:30	
	:45	
5	:00	
	:30	
6	:00	
	:30	
7	:00	
	:30	
8	:00	
	:30	
9	:00	
	:30	

Date: [ ]   Start Day: [ ]

Day:

_____

		Reminders
-		
-		
-		
-		
-		
-		
-		
-		
-		
-		

☑	ABC	Prioritized Task List

Time	People to Call

$Amt	Expenses

Appointments

7 :00	
:30	
8 :00	
:15	
:30	
:45	
9 :00	
:15	
:30	
:45	
10 :00	
:15	
:30	
:45	
11 :00	
:15	
:30	
:45	
12 :00	
:15	
:30	
:45	
1 :00	
:15	
:30	
:45	
2 :00	
:15	
:30	
:45	
3 :00	
:15	
:30	
:45	
4 :00	
:15	
:30	
:45	
5 :00	
:30	
6 :00	
:30	
7 :00	
:30	
8 :00	
:30	
9 :00	
:30	

Week Beginning: [   ]

Month:

_____

Important

Notes

Monday

1
2
3
4
5
6
7
8
9
10
11

Tuesday

1
2
3
4
5
6
7
8
9
10
11

☑	ABC	**Prioritized Task List**

Wednesday

1
2
3
4
5
6
7
8
9
10
11

Thursday

1
2
3
4
5
6
7
8
9
10
11

Friday

1
2
3
4
5
6
7
8
9
10
11

Saturday

1
2
3
4
5
6

Sunday

1
2
3
4
5
6

Date	**People to Call**

Date: [ ]   Start Day: [ ]

Day:

Reminders
-
-
-
-
-
-
-
-
-

☑	ABC	Prioritized Task List

Time	People to Call

$Amt	Expenses

Appointments	
7 :00	
:30	
8 :00	
:15	
:30	
:45	
9 :00	
:15	
:30	
:45	
10 :00	
:15	
:30	
:45	
11 :00	
:15	
:30	
:45	
12 :00	
:15	
:30	
:45	
1 :00	
:15	
:30	
:45	
2 :00	
:15	
:30	
:45	
3 :00	
:15	
:30	
:45	
4 :00	
:15	
:30	
:45	
5 :00	
:30	
6 :00	
:30	
7 :00	
:30	
8 :00	
:30	
9 :00	
:30	

Date: [   ]   Start Day: [   ]

Day:

Reminders
-
-
-
-
-
-
-
-
-
-

☑	ABC	Prioritized Task List

Time	People to Call

$Amt	Expenses

Appointments	
7 :00	
:30	
8 :00	
:15	
:30	
:45	
9 :00	
:15	
:30	
:45	
10 :00	
:15	
:30	
:45	
11 :00	
:15	
:30	
:45	
12 :00	
:15	
:30	
:45	
1 :00	
:15	
:30	
:45	
2 :00	
:15	
:30	
:45	
3 :00	
:15	
:30	
:45	
4 :00	
:15	
:30	
:45	
5 :00	
:30	
6 :00	
:30	
7 :00	
:30	
8 :00	
:30	
9 :00	
:30	

Daily Planner

Date: [　　　]   Start Day: [　　　　]

Day:

_____

Reminders

- _____
- _____
- _____
- _____
- _____
- _____
- _____
- _____
- _____
- _____

☑	ABC	Prioritized Task List

Time	People to Call

$Amt	Expenses

Appointments

Time	
7:00	
:30	
8:00	
:15	
:30	
:45	
9:00	
:15	
:30	
:45	
10:00	
:15	
:30	
:45	
11:00	
:15	
:30	
:45	
12:00	
:15	
:30	
:45	
1:00	
:15	
:30	
:45	
2:00	
:15	
:30	
:45	
3:00	
:15	
:30	
:45	
4:00	
:15	
:30	
:45	
5:00	
:30	
6:00	
:30	
7:00	
:30	
8:00	
:30	
9:00	
:30	

Date: [　　　　]　　　　　　Start Day: [　　　　　　　]

Day:

Reminders
-
-
-
-
-
-
-
-
-
-

☑	ABC	**Prioritized Task List**

Time	**People to Call**

$Amt	**Expenses**

	Appointments
7 :00	
:30	
8 :00	
:15	
:30	
:45	
9 :00	
:15	
:30	
:45	
10 :00	
:15	
:30	
:45	
11 :00	
:15	
:30	
:45	
12 :00	
:15	
:30	
:45	
1 :00	
:15	
:30	
:45	
2 :00	
:15	
:30	
:45	
3 :00	
:15	
:30	
:45	
4 :00	
:15	
:30	
:45	
5 :00	
:30	
6 :00	
:30	
7 :00	
:30	
8 :00	
:30	
9 :00	
:30	

Date: [ ]   Start Day: [ ]

Day:

	Reminders
-	
-	
-	
-	
-	
-	
-	
-	
-	

☑	ABC	Prioritized Task List

Time	People to Call

$Amt	Expenses

Appointments

7 :00	
:30	
8 :00	
:15	
:30	
:45	
9 :00	
:15	
:30	
:45	
10 :00	
:15	
:30	
:45	
11 :00	
:15	
:30	
:45	
12 :00	
:15	
:30	
:45	
1 :00	
:15	
:30	
:45	
2 :00	
:15	
:30	
:45	
3 :00	
:15	
:30	
:45	
4 :00	
:15	
:30	
:45	
5 :00	
:30	
6 :00	
:30	
7 :00	
:30	
8 :00	
:30	
9 :00	
:30	

Date: [____]   Start Day: [_____]

Day:

_____

	Reminders
-	_____
-	_____
-	_____
-	_____
-	_____
-	_____
-	_____
-	_____
-	_____
-	_____

☑	ABC	Prioritized Task List

Time	People to Call

$Amt	Expenses

Appointments

7 :00	
:30	
8 :00	
:15	
:30	
:45	
9 :00	
:15	
:30	
:45	
10 :00	
:15	
:30	
:45	
11 :00	
:15	
:30	
:45	
12 :00	
:15	
:30	
:45	
1 :00	
:15	
:30	
:45	
2 :00	
:15	
:30	
:45	
3 :00	
:15	
:30	
:45	
4 :00	
:15	
:30	
:45	
5 :00	
:30	
6 :00	
:30	
7 :00	
:30	
8 :00	
:30	
9 :00	
:30	

Date: ☐　　　　　　　Start Day: ☐

Day:

Reminders
-
-
-
-
-
-
-
-
-
-

☑	ABC	Prioritized Task List

Time	People to Call

$Amt	Expenses

	Appointments
7 :00	
:30	
8 :00	
:15	
:30	
:45	
9 :00	
:15	
:30	
:45	
10 :00	
:15	
:30	
:45	
11 :00	
:15	
:30	
:45	
12 :00	
:15	
:30	
:45	
1 :00	
:15	
:30	
:45	
2 :00	
:15	
:30	
:45	
3 :00	
:15	
:30	
:45	
4 :00	
:15	
:30	
:45	
5 :00	
:30	
6 :00	
:30	
7 :00	
:30	
8 :00	
:30	
9 :00	
:30	

Weekly Planner

Week Beginning: [   ]

Important

Month:

_____

Notes
_____
_____
_____
_____
_____
_____
_____
_____
_____
_____
_____
_____
_____
_____

Monday
1 _____
2 _____
3 _____
4 _____
5 _____
6 _____
7 _____
8 _____
9 _____
10 _____
11 _____

Tuesday
1 _____
2 _____
3 _____
4 _____
5 _____
6 _____
7 _____
8 _____
9 _____
10 _____
11 _____

☑	ABC	Prioritized Task List

Wednesday
_____
_____
1 _____
2 _____
3 _____
4 _____
5 _____
6 _____
7 _____
8 _____
9 _____
10 _____
11 _____

Thursday
_____
_____
1 _____
2 _____
3 _____
4 _____
5 _____
6 _____
7 _____
8 _____
9 _____
10 _____
11 _____

Friday
1 _____
2 _____
3 _____
4 _____
5 _____
6 _____
7 _____
8 _____
9 _____
10 _____
11 _____

Saturday
_____
_____
1 _____
2 _____
3 _____
4 _____
5 _____
6 _____

Sunday
1 _____
2 _____
3 _____
4 _____
5 _____
6 _____

Date	People to Call

Date: [ ]   Start Day: [ ]

Day:

	Reminders
-	
-	
-	
-	
-	
-	
-	
-	
-	

☑	ABC	Prioritized Task List

Time	People to Call

$Amt	Expenses

	Appointments
7 :00	
:30	
8 :00	
:15	
:30	
:45	
9 :00	
:15	
:30	
:45	
10 :00	
:15	
:30	
:45	
11 :00	
:15	
:30	
:45	
12 :00	
:15	
:30	
:45	
1 :00	
:15	
:30	
:45	
2 :00	
:15	
:30	
:45	
3 :00	
:15	
:30	
:45	
4 :00	
:15	
:30	
:45	
5 :00	
:30	
6 :00	
:30	
7 :00	
:30	
8 :00	
:30	
9 :00	
:30	

Date: ☐   Start Day: ☐

Day:

Reminders
-
-
-
-
-
-
-
-
-
-

☑	ABC	Prioritized Task List

Time	People to Call

$Amt	Expenses

Appointments	
7 :00	
:30	
8 :00	
:15	
:30	
:45	
9 :00	
:15	
:30	
:45	
10 :00	
:15	
:30	
:45	
11 :00	
:15	
:30	
:45	
12 :00	
:15	
:30	
:45	
1 :00	
:15	
:30	
:45	
2 :00	
:15	
:30	
:45	
3 :00	
:15	
:30	
:45	
4 :00	
:15	
:30	
:45	
5 :00	
:30	
6 :00	
:30	
7 :00	
:30	
8 :00	
:30	
9 :00	
:30	

Date: [ ]　　　　　　　Start Day: [ ]

Day:

Reminders
-
-
-
-
-
-
-
-
-

☑	ABC	Prioritized Task List

Time	People to Call

$Amt	Expenses

Appointments

7	:00	
	:30	
8	:00	
	:15	
	:30	
	:45	
9	:00	
	:15	
	:30	
	:45	
10	:00	
	:15	
	:30	
	:45	
11	:00	
	:15	
	:30	
	:45	
12	:00	
	:15	
	:30	
	:45	
1	:00	
	:15	
	:30	
	:45	
2	:00	
	:15	
	:30	
	:45	
3	:00	
	:15	
	:30	
	:45	
4	:00	
	:15	
	:30	
	:45	
5	:00	
	:30	
6	:00	
	:30	
7	:00	
	:30	
8	:00	
	:30	
9	:00	
	:30	

Date: [   ]   Start Day: [   ]

Day:

Reminders
-
-
-
-
-
-
-
-
-
-

☑	ABC	Prioritized Task List

Time	People to Call

$Amt	Expenses

Appointments	
7 :00	
:30	
8 :00	
:15	
:30	
:45	
9 :00	
:15	
:30	
:45	
10 :00	
:15	
:30	
:45	
11 :00	
:15	
:30	
:45	
12 :00	
:15	
:30	
:45	
1 :00	
:15	
:30	
:45	
2 :00	
:15	
:30	
:45	
3 :00	
:15	
:30	
:45	
4 :00	
:15	
:30	
:45	
5 :00	
:30	
6 :00	
:30	
7 :00	
:30	
8 :00	
:30	
9 :00	
:30	

Date: ☐   Start Day: ☐

Day:

Reminders
-
-
-
-
-
-
-
-
-

☑	ABC	**Prioritized Task List**

Time	People to Call

$Amt	Expenses

Appointments

7	:00	
	:30	
8	:00	
	:15	
	:30	
	:45	
9	:00	
	:15	
	:30	
	:45	
10	:00	
	:15	
	:30	
	:45	
11	:00	
	:15	
	:30	
	:45	
12	:00	
	:15	
	:30	
	:45	
1	:00	
	:15	
	:30	
	:45	
2	:00	
	:15	
	:30	
	:45	
3	:00	
	:15	
	:30	
	:45	
4	:00	
	:15	
	:30	
	:45	
5	:00	
	:30	
6	:00	
	:30	
7	:00	
	:30	
8	:00	
	:30	
9	:00	
	:30	

Date: [   ]   Start Day: [   ]

Day:

Reminders
-
-
-
-
-
-
-
-
-
-

☑	ABC	Prioritized Task List

Time	People to Call

$Amt	Expenses

	Appointments
7 :00	
:30	
8 :00	
:15	
:30	
:45	
9 :00	
:15	
:30	
:45	
10 :00	
:15	
:30	
:45	
11 :00	
:15	
:30	
:45	
12 :00	
:15	
:30	
:45	
1 :00	
:15	
:30	
:45	
2 :00	
:15	
:30	
:45	
3 :00	
:15	
:30	
:45	
4 :00	
:15	
:30	
:45	
5 :00	
:30	
6 :00	
:30	
7 :00	
:30	
8 :00	
:30	
9 :00	
:30	

Date: [   ]   Start Day: [   ]

Day:

_____

Reminders
-
-
-
-
-
-
-
-
-

☑	ABC	Prioritized Task List

Time	People to Call

$Amt	Expenses

Appointments

Time	
7 :00	
:30	
8 :00	
:15	
:30	
:45	
9 :00	
:15	
:30	
:45	
10 :00	
:15	
:30	
:45	
11 :00	
:15	
:30	
:45	
12 :00	
:15	
:30	
:45	
1 :00	
:15	
:30	
:45	
2 :00	
:15	
:30	
:45	
3 :00	
:15	
:30	
:45	
4 :00	
:15	
:30	
:45	
5 :00	
:30	
6 :00	
:30	
7 :00	
:30	
8 :00	
:30	
9 :00	
:30	

Client Contact Information:

Name	Address	Phone Number